GARDEN POOLS

by

PAUL STETSON

PARADISE WATER GARDENS

Distributed in the U.S.A. by T.F.H. Publications, Inc., 211 West Sylvania Avenue, P.O. Box 27, Neptune City, N.J. 07753; in England by T.F.H. (Gt. Britain) Ltd., 13 Nutley Lane, Reigate, Surrey; in Canada to the book store and library trade by Clarke, Irwin & Company, Clarwin House, 791 St. Clair Avenue West, Toronto 10, Ontario; in Canada to the pet trade by Rolf C. Hagen Ltd., 3225 Sartelon Street, Montreal 382, Quebec; in Southeast Asia by Y.W. Ong, 9 Lorong 36 Geylang, Singapore 14; in Australia and the south Pacific by Pet Imports Pty. Ltd., P.O. Box 149, Brookvale 2100, N.S.W., Australia. Published by T.F.H. Publications, Inc. Ltd., The British Crown Colony of Hong Kong.

ISBN 0-87666-077-4

CONTENTS

The author with an Aqua Lite Pool.

A beautiful informal garden pool enhances the landscape. Photo by Laurence E. Perkins.

INTRODUCTION

Water and the creatures that live in it, both plant and animal, have fascinated mankind for thousands of years. Part of this fascination is attributable to water's important part in our scheme of things, but an even more important part is the direct result of water's capacity to nurture life. What lives in water may be large or small, peaceful or vicious, useful or useless. Many times it is beautiful, and it is always interesting, even to the insensitive.

These two things, beauty and interest, account for the popularity of water gardening, a popularity that is yearly growing greater as more homeowners come to the realization that a water garden on their property is a source of satisfaction that can be matched by no other decorative feature. A properly maintained water garden is beautiful and provocative of interest; it is a joy to watch and a joy to care for. A garden pool can change the most prosaic landscape into a fairyland of enchantment, and its rewards far outweigh the small expense and effort involved in its creation and upkeep. On a more practical plane, there is another consideration: a water garden can add substantially to the value of your property.

Moreover, the pleasures of owning a water garden are not restricted to only a few, for water gardens can be tailored to your pocketbook and ambition. If you have a lot of money to spend and really want to do it up brown, you can, but you don't have to, because a small pool can in its own way be as satisfying as a larger one. If you want to spend a lot, okay; if you want to spend only a little, that's okay too. It's your decision to make.

We are interested in this book in water gardening primarily from the standpoint of discussing the purchase of garden pools and the choice of plants for these pools, although attention will also be given to constructing pools and to those animals which have come to be associated with pools and make fine companions for the plants. In their own ways, plants and animals work together to give garden pools the amalgam of beauty and interest which has been their source

The beautiful flowers of the hardy lily James Brydon, after a shower. Photo by Laurence E. Perkins.

Nymphaea species proliferate in a large pool bordered by rushes. Photo by Duncan Sculthorpe.

of popularity. Each adds something to the whole. Of course, it is not a strict necessity to have both; if your tastes dictate that plants alone are to populate your pool, that's all you need.

I have concentrated on the practical aspects of water gardening, the things that are of most value to beginners in the hobby. Where technical information is presented it is given in digestible form. There is nothing occult about water gardening. If you apply yourself to the mastery of sound principles you are bound to succeed. Some will succeed better than others, as is to be expected in any undertaking, but *everyone* can succeed. I hope here to show you how.

The pads of these lilies almost completely cover the surface of the pond. Photo by Duncan Sculthorpe.

WHAT IS WATER GARDENING?

Water gardening is that form of the horticultural hobby which is concerned with the growth and propagation of plants that live in water. As such, water gardening is simply gardening with water, and a water garden is a garden in which water, not soil, is the largest single factor. Now I do not mean to say by this that a water garden uses no soil, nor that water gardening is more akin to hydroponics than to the culture of terrestrial plants. It is gardening, but gardening of a different type. It is, like terrestrial gardening, a hobby, a nature hobby. Where some people predisposed toward an interest in nature choose to use animals such as tropical fishes and guinea pigs and birds and turtles as their source of enjoyment of nature and her mysteries, the gardener uses plants for the same purpose, and the water gardener chooses special plants, aquatic and semi-aquatic plants, for his. A person chooses to be a water gardener for the same reason that a stamp collector begins collecting stamps or a bird watcher starts watching birds: he thinks he'll like it.

A garden, be it water or terrestrial, must contain plants. It can hold cacti or peonies or roses or even tomatoes, but it must contain something. A water garden contains water plants; these may be either strictly aquatic or only semi-aquatic. Since the most beautiful, and consequently the most popular, plants for garden pools are water lilies, I'll discuss them in greatest detail. From a practical standpoint, water gardening is water lily gardening. However, water lilies are not the only plants adapted to life in a garden pool, so I'll also discuss other types of aquatic plants commonly found in garden pools.

So now we know what water gardening is, and from this we can see that two of the most important elements in a garden pool are the plants and the pool itself. Let's take them up one by one.

GARDEN POOLS . . . THEIR CONSTRUCTION AND CARE

Since individuals differ in their tastes and their abilities to satisfy these tastes, garden pools come in a variety of shapes, sizes, and materials. Broadly speaking, there are two main types of pools: prefabricated and made to order. Either type can well serve the purpose for which it is intended, and the choice of material, size, and shape depends mainly on how much you want to spend. Generally, specially constructed pools, those made to your specifications and designed so as to maximize their beautifying effect on the property on which they are located, are by far the most expensive, although they are naturally the most satisfying. They are generally also the largest and most ornate.

Prefabricated or preconstructed pools cost less and are easier to install, since the installation process usually consists of no more than digging a hole and inserting the ready-made pool. The most popular materials for these pools are fiberglass and heavy plastic, both of which are impervious to the weather and can stand the formation of winter ice. These pools come in sizes ranging from 4 to 14 feet across at prices from about $50 to $250. Presently on the market is a kidney-shaped flexible polyethylene pool measuring 48 by 38 inches across the top and 12 inches deep. This pool, called Aqua Lite, can be purchased separately or as a complete unit with plants and plant foods, fish, etc., for about $22. Admirably suited to beginners who would like to try water gardening without getting their feet wet in the financial sense, it is available from water garden suppliers.

With either fabricated or constructed pools, one point is of major importance: location. Water lilies need as much daylight as you can give them, so locate your pool in the sunniest spot available, free from shade. In addition, it is best to have the pool located on ground raised a little above the elevation of the rest of the garden, if possible, as this prevents flooding and allows for better drainage.

Concrete pools are the most popular of the constructed pools. These concrete pools fall into two general categories: formal and informal. The formal pool is one which makes no attempt to look as if it had been made by nature. It is specially constructed, and it looks it. Formal pools are regular in shape and generally the largest of all garden pools. The informal pool is designed to look as if it were the result of water casually deposited by natural methods. It is irregular in outline and generally smaller than the formal pool.

The larger the pond, the larger the lilies that may be used. The many large *Nymphaea* species in this pond are not crowded, as they have room to spread out. Photo by Duncan Sculthorpe.

Construction of either of these types of pools requires specialized skills, and I do not recommend that you try to build your own pool. It is in most cases easier and a lot cheaper in the long run to entrust the work (and it is real work, not just play) to professionals who will do the job quickly and efficiently. This applies especially to the construction of formal pools, if only because the construction of an informal pool, or at least its final form, is a matter of individual expression. My advice is to leave the work to those best qualified to do it, but I offer the following suggestions as a general guide to those who care to give it a try.

Before construction, first outline an area a little larger than the proposed area of your pool; a garden hose will be helpful here. When excavating, bowl out the pool; that is, slope it gradually so that ice will be able to expand without meeting too much resistance from the concrete sides of the pool. After the pool has been dug, place a layer of pea stone over the entire exposed area, and then shape chicken wire into the completed contour. The pool is now ready for its first layer of cement, which should be 2 to 3 inches thick. Allow the layer to settle for a day, and then apply a finish coat composed of 1 part very fine sand and 1 part Portland cement. Formal, straight-sided pools require additional reinforcement with steel rods and usually require the use of forms into which the concrete is poured, since the walls of such a pool must be much thicker, between 6 and 10 inches. The best mix for cementing a pool is composed of 2 parts of pea stone (not over $\frac{1}{2}''$), 3 parts washed sand, and 1 part Portland cement. I consider a drain useless, unless you can connect it directly to your sewage system or to a lower drainage level that will not back up.

Make sure that your pool is deep enough, at least 20 inches but not more than 36 inches, to bring it to below the frost line and allow it to serve as a permanent home for all hardy water lily varieties to survive the winter below the ice. This is necessary, for all water lilies, both tropical and hardy, will die if the crown of the plant is frozen. Goldfish and some other aquatic animals also can survive over the winter if the pool is deep enough.

You must also be careful to see to it that the pool is properly cured before you introduce your plants or animals. The cement in a new pool has a highly alkalizing effect on the water, rendering it unsafe for both plants and fishes. In order to allow the water to leach out all the alkali, you must fill the pool, allow the water to stand for a week, and then completely empty and refill the pool three more times, allowing the water to stand a week between each refilling. Be patient; once properly cured, the pool will never have to be cured again, unless it is cemented again. Don't paint your pool until the curing process is completed, and be careful in the type of paint selected; some are fatally toxic. Ask your plant supplier; he has the right types. Rockery will greatly enhance and naturalize your pool. Flat stones at the pool's edge will set it off beautifully and allow the use of many low-growing 'nnuals and perennials, such as Allysum and Ground Phlox. Shrubbery and taller plants should be planted only to the north of the pool, to lessen their shading effect. Fountains and waterfalls further enhance your pool; now that submersible water pumps are available, you can easily clean and recirculate the same water over and over and still get the effect of constant running water. This is especially valuable if fishes are to be kept in the pool. Feather rock, only a quarter as heavy as fieldstone, can be formed into beautiful bases of fountains and waterfalls. It is readily available at about 15¢ per pound. Water pumps are priced at from $15.00 to $50.00 each.

Formal pools like the one shown here are regular in outline. Photo by Laurence E Perkins.

Both formal and informal lily pools will accent any garden and, in fact, become the focal point. Japanese gardens, among the most beautiful in the world, would not be complete without a garden pool. Bird watchers will delight in the way their pools attract more birds than ever before.

Several types of hardy bamboo are most adaptable in landscaping around your pool. Arched bridges over large pools or natural pools are most appealing. Stone lanterns are in good taste, and frog and flamingo ornaments will add to your surroundings. Water lilies are the most photogenic of flowers and make the most beautiful of all color slides. I often gaze upon them during the winter months and become spellbound by their color and beauty.

VARIETIES OF WATER LILIES

Water lilies, which range in size from the miniature Madagascar lilies, with leaves only two inches across, to the mammoth *Victoria regia*, with leaves large and strong enough to support the weight of a child, are divided for the purpose of water gardeners into two main classes, hardy lilies and tropical lilies, and the tropical lilies are further divided into two groupings, day-blooming and night-blooming, which names are self-explanatory.

We'll deal mostly with the hardy lilies, most of which were developed by the Frenchman Marliac, whose genius and secrets died with him. Marliac developed nearly all of the hardy hybrid varieties popular today. The tropical lilies were developed mainly by George Pring, Director of the Missouri Botanical Gardens, where, at Tower Park, he developed dozens of outstandingly beautiful water lily varieties.

The hardy water lilies are those which withstand the winter in areas in which a pool normally becomes frozen over during the winter months. These lilies propagate vegetatively, by division of matured plants. Three miniature hardy water lilies well suited to the garden pool are *Nymphaea tetragona*, native to most of northern America, *Nymphaea mexicana*, and a sport of *Nymphaea tetragona* known as

The large leaves of *Victoria regia* can support a child's weight. Photo by A. M. Friedrich.

14

These South American water plants have had to adapt to crowded conditions in their home waters. Photo by Harald Schultz.

Joanne Pring, with deep pink petals. These lilies are ideal for tub culture, since they require little room. Their flowers are tiny, only 2 inches in diameter; these lilies bloom from spring until heavy frost.

Closely related to the plants of the genus *Nymphaea* are the plants of the genus *Nelumbo*, the water lotuses. There are three colors to be had in lotus varieties: white (Asiatic), yellow (American), and pink (Egyptian).

This last mentioned lotus is the sacred lotus of the Nile. There is also a rare double lotus, called Shiorman, from China. The flower of the water lotus is most fragrant, and the plant has exceedingly attractive ruffled leaves that stand above the level of the water. Water lotuses may be considered hardy if protected. They will, in fact, often overrun natural ponds when not controlled.

Interest in the tropical *Nymphaea* species became intense right after the turn of the century, and since 1912 many outstanding varieties have been developed. Temperatures lower than 70° will cause these tropical lilies to go dormant, so in northern latitudes they cannot be planted outdoors until real summer weather begins, usually at least late June. These lilies are grown indoors in greenhouses starting in February and are fully developed plants, usually in bloom, at planting time. Three new outstanding varieties have been developed

15

by Martin Randig of California. These are Evelyn Randig, rose red with maroon and green leaves; Trail Blazer, a brilliant yellow; and Afterglow, a bright new talisman shade. Since tropical lilies cannot be wintered out they must be treated as annuals, and it is usually advisable to purchase fresh plants each spring. The method I use to propagate tropical water lilies is to dig the plants after the first frost and remove from the base of the mother tuber the small tuber that has formed. These are stored in moist sand until spring, at which time they are placed in heated concrete tanks where they yield young plants which will develop into finished blooming-size plants in about 3 months. These plants will bloom all summer until severe frost. Tropical lilies have a much longer blooming season than hardies. Some varieties of lilies are viviparous; that is, young plants sprout out of the centers of the parent leaves. Of course, all of the fine hybrids were propagated from seed.

Unlike hardy water lilies, there are several fine varieties of night-blooming *Nymphaea* species, such as H. C. Haarstick, red; E. G. Hutchings, a bright pink; and Missouri, white. These varieties bloom from late afternoon into the following morning.

Leaves and flower of "Madam Wilfon Gonnere", a giant double water lily. Photo by Duncan Sculthorpe.

16

Closeup of the fringed water lily, *Nymphoides peltata*, showing shaggy margins of the petals. Photo by Duncan Sculthorpe.

There are also two miniature blue tropical day-blooming lilies, Colarata and the highly prolific Madagascar Dwarf, the small plants of which are often used as aquarium plants.

One other lily variety not to be overlooked is the interesting Water Platter discovered by a Spanish botanist in 1801 in the tributaries of the Amazon. It was later discovered again in British Guiana and sent to England to be named after Queen Victoria, and thus became known as *Victoria regia*. Its upturned leaves are capable of sustaining great weight and will support a child weighing 50 pounds. Flowers are white and measure up to 14 inches across. Propagation is by seed, and a pool not less than 20 feet in diameter is necessary to accommodate one of these plants. Unfortunately, it is not always available.

Listed here are what in my opinion are some of the best varieties of hardy and tropical water lilies.

HARDY LILIES

REDS

ESCARBOUCLE (Marliac 1910) the most brilliantly colored red lily.

GLORIOSA (Marliac 1896). The most popular red in view of its moderate growth and profusion of blooms. Ideal for small pools.

JAMES BRYDON (Dreer). Also very popular, somewhat larger than Gloriosa, free blooming and fragrant.

ATTRACTION (Marliac 1910). Deep red, a very large lily not suited for small pool culture.

PINK SHADES

PINK OPAL (Fowler 1915). Deep pink and highly fragrant, well suited for small pool culture.

HELEN FOWLER (Shaw). Deep rose pink, having large free-blooming flowers. Medium in growth and moderately priced.

PINK SENSATION. Perhaps the finest of the newer varieties of water lilies.

DELICATE PINK. Free flowering. Blooms early and closes late. A must for the real fancier.

ROSE ARREY (Fowler 1913). Deep cerise pink, having blooms up to 7 inches across. Recommended for larger pools.

YELLOW SHADES

CROMATELLA (Marliac). Rich yellow medium-size flowers borne in profusion, plus moderate growth, make this lily our most popular seller. Bronze markings set off its green leaves. Ideal for small and large pools.

SUNRISE (origin unknown). Has canary yellow flowers up to 10 inches across. The largest of the hardy lilies. Suited to medium and larger pools. Most spectacular if you have the room.

CHANGEABLES

COMANCHE (Marliac 1908). Large rich apricot flower that changes to orange flowing with red as the flower ages. Suited to medium and larger pools.

PAUL HARIOT (Marliac 1905). Similar in color changes to Comanche but much more moderate in growth. Ideal for small pool culture.

AURORA (Marliac 1895). Opens a creamy yellow, changing to orange and then to red. Suited to small pool culture. A real novelty.

WHITES

MARLIAC WHITE (Marliac 1880). Free blooming, best white with very fragrant blooms. Very vigorous growing. Medium to large pools.

GONNERE (Marliac 1914). One of the few truly double water lilies. Flower resembles pure white snowballs floating on the water. Ideal for small pools.

GLADSTONE (Richardson). A very large white lily. A shy bloomer unless given plenty of room.

HARDY PYGMY WATER LILIES

DWARF WHITE. Native to North America, the smallest of all water lilies.

TETRAGONA HELVOLA. A tiny yellow introduced by Marliac. Ideal for miniature pools.

JOANNE PRING. A pink sport which first appeared in 1942. Flowers are 2 inches across and are deep pink, free-blooming, and well adapted to miniature water gardens.

All of the above varieties are readily available.

TROPICAL WATER LILIES—DAY-BLOOMING
WHITE

MRS. GEORGE PRING (Pring 1922). A pure white lily with fragrant blooms up to 12 inches in diameter. Adapts to smaller pools.

ISABELLE PRING (1941). Cream color counterpart to the above white.

YELLOW SHADES

TRAIL BLAZER (Randig). A recent introduction that rivals all other tropicals. The most brilliant yellow yet produced. Adapts to most pools.

ST. LOUIS (Pring 1932). The first patented water lily and the largest flowering yellow tropical.

BLUE SHADES AND PURPLES

BAGDAD (Pring 1941). Wisteria blue in color, with leaves that have the appearance of a Persian rug with a red, brown, and green pattern. A favorite.

DIRECTOR MOORE (Pring 1941). I consider this lily the best of the blues because of its moderate growth and its profusion of dark blue flowers. Ideal for all pools.

BLUE BEAUTY (Tricker 1897). Light blue with large fragrant flowers. One of the most popular lilies among tropicals. Highly recommended.

LEOPARDUS (Randig). Wisteria blue with most spectacular foliage, spotted with maroon against green. A recent introduction well worth trying.

MRS. EDWARD WHITTAKER (Pring 1917). A gigantic light blue lily adaptable only to large pools, where it becomes a water show piece.

ROYAL PURPLE (Buskirk). A moderate-growing purple water lily. Ideal for small pools.

PANAMA PACIFIC (Tricker). Plum purple and very prolific; fragrant and free blooming. Ideal for pools of all sizes. Viviparous.

PINK SHADES

AMERICAN BEAUTY (Pring 1941). The nearest to red among day blooming tropicals. Adapts to most pool sizes. Not always available.

GENERAL PERSHING (Pring 1917). A very popular pink tropical. A deep pink that adapts to smaller pools but if given the room will develop considerable size. Fragrant and free blooming.

GOLDEN WEST (Randig). Large flowering peach pink; very fragrant and most prolific.

AFTERGLOW (Randig). One of the finest hybrids of the 20th century. Coloration much like that of a talisman rose but very glowing in appearance.

EVELYN RANDIG (Randig). A rich glowing rose red variety having spotted leaves that are green and maroon. Very showy. A recent introduction.

DWARF DAY-BLOOMING TROPICAL LILY

DAUBEN. A German introduction and the smallest of the tropicals. A tremendous bloomer with light blue flowers up to 3 inches in diameter. Very prolific; the young plants are often sold as indoor aquarium plants. Viviparous.

NIGHT-BLOOMING TROPICALS

E. G. HUTCHINGS (Gurney). A very large flowering night-bloomer with deep pink petals. The leaves are undulating and bronze in color.

H. C. HAARSTICK (Gurney). The most popular night-bloomer and the most red tropical lily. The leaves are dark coppery red and it is free blooming.

MISSOURI (Pring 1933). This lily under proper conditions will bear enormous white flowers up to 14 inches across and needs a pool of considerable size to properly develop, although as with most tropical lilies it will confine itself within its limits. Has sharply undulating bronze pads.

VICTORIA. Colossal aquatic giant adapted to only the largest of pools and only where the season is long. Grown only from seed, with white flowers and gigantic leaves. Occasional availability.

Nelumbium speciosum, the sacred lotus of the Nile. Photo by Duncan Sculthorpe.

LOTUS

American-Yellow flowers with leaves growing out of water, forming decorative counterpart to water lilies.

LOTUS-ASIATIC—*White*   LOTUS-ROSEUM BLENUM—*double pink*

LOTUS-EGYPTIAN—*Pink*   LOTUS-SHIROMAN—*double white*

There are over twenty recognized species in shades of red, pink, yellow, and white. Those mentioned are the most popular.

PLANTING AND CARE OF WATER LILIES

Although hardy and tropical lilies differ in many respects, both varieties have the same planting requirements. Both types are heavy feeders requiring a compost rich in decomposed organic material. Tropical lilies to be grown in a single season should be planted in a pot or tub at least 10 inches in diameter containing a compost of 2/3 garden soil and 1/3 well rotted cow manure or a cup of commercial water lily fertilizer, a highly organic formulation. Commercial fertilizer is better than the cow manure because it encourages the growth of algae less. A supplemental mid-summer feeding should be given in July; this can be done by placing the fertilizer in cheesecloth and forcing it in around the plants. At the time of planting at least 1 inch of gravel should be placed over the compost, and the crown of the lily should be allowed to show slightly above the level of the gravel.

When the lily is first introduced into the pond there will be a setback in growth. This is a natural consequence of transplanting and nothing to be alarmed about; it is rare that a good sound root will fail to grow, and most reputable suppliers will guarantee that your plant will grow, provided it gets plenty of sunshine.

Hybrid lilies are more satisfactory than native lilies and will bloom more profusely. Most water lilies can be bought for between $2.00 and $6.00; the hardy varieties, like shrubbery, will afford pleasure for many years. Although tropical lilies must generally be replaced each year, almost everyone who has experience with them finds it worthwhile to replace them each summer. Blue is the preferred color in tropical lilies, one reason for this being that there are no blue hardy lilies.

Besides lilies, there are many other interesting and reasonably priced plants which should be added to your pool. Among these, Water Hyacinths are popular, for they are both beautiful and useful in cutting down on algal growth in the pool. *Elodea* (Anacharis) and *Cabomba* are cheap but pretty plants which may be used in the pool either planted or floating. *Cabomba*, as a matter of fact, is a water lily itself, belonging to the plant family Nymphaeacae. *Vallisneria* and *Sagittaria* are grasslike plants which must be planted, although they do not need soil but can be planted in plain gravel. Other plants, such as Cattail, Flowering Rush, Arrowhead, Sweet Flag, and Cardinal

A view of a tropical pool, showing Water Hyacinth (foreground and middle), *Nymphaea* species (left,) and *Nelumbium speciosum* (extreme right). Photo by Duncan Sculthorpe.

The fertilizer is mixed into rich garden soil contained in a 10-inch tub. Use one cup of fertilizer per tub, and stir well into the soil. Photo by Paul Stetson.

Place the lily into the half-filled pot. Photo by Paul Stetson.

Build soil up around the lily to the level of the plant's crown. Photo by Paul Stetson.

Place an inch of gravel over the entire surface of the pot to prevent roiling of the soil-fertilizer mixture when the pot is placed into the water. The lily is now ready to be put into the pool. Photo by Paul Stetson.

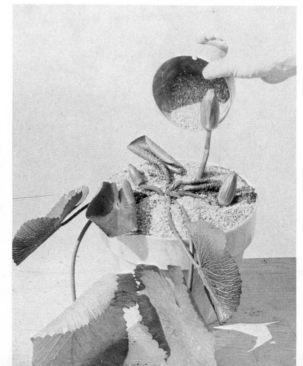

Vallisneria can be planted in gravel; it needs no soil in order to take root. Photo by Laurence E. Perkins.

Sagittaria is another rooted plant which will be welcome in the pool. Photo by Laurence E. Perkins.

Cabomba, which may be used rooted or floating, is cheap but attractive. Photo by Duncan Sculthorpe.

Flower, all of which are hardy plants, are easily available and moderately priced, much below the price of water lilies. Tropical plants such as Umbrella Palm, Papyrus, Taro, Water Snowflake, Water Poppy, Yellow Calla and Caladium make a charming array of shallow water plants.

A rhizome of the hardy lily "Attraction", with leaf development. This is the proper planting position for this lily. The section beyond the root growth may be removed before planting. Photo by Paul Stetson.

This specimen of E. G. Hutchings is ready to be potted and introduced to the pool. This plant is almost three months old and in full bud stage. Photo by Paul Stetson.

A tuber of the night-blooming H. C. Haarstick, showing two young lilies ready to be planted in 5-inch pots. Photo by Paul Stetson.

A tuber of the lily Evelyn Randig; this tuber will yield several plants more. Photo by Paul Stetson.

29

GOLDFISH AND OTHER POOL ANIMALS

Besides the plants, the pool should also include frogs and tadpoles, snails, turtles, and salamanders. All of these add interest and are entertaining, and they serve useful purposes. Tadpoles, for instance, are good scavengers, and all of these aquatic animals, with the exception of snails, will eat mosquito larvae or any other unwelcome insect larvae which is deposited in your pool. But of course the most welcome animals in your pool are fishes, and the most welcome fishes are Goldfish (*Carassius auratus*) and Koi, another fancy Carp.

There are many varieties of Goldfish suitable for your pool, including Shubunkins, with their multitude of colors, even blue; Calico Fans, with three-cornered tails; Black Moors, with telescope

Tadpoles can be valuable scavengers in the pool. This is a tadpole of a bullfrog. Photo courtesy of the American Museum of Natural History.

Goldfish can be conditioned to come to a certain spot in the pool to be fed. Photo by Laurence E. Perkins.

Salamanders add interest and novelty to the pool. Photo by Dr. Herbert R. Axelrod.

eyes; and popular and hardy Comets and Commons. Rare Goldfish like the Lionhead and Oranda are not hardy enough to live in the pool through the winter, but they make nice showpieces and may be wintered in an indoor aquarium. Native fishes are not recommended, as they are usually aggressive or drab, or both. The Golden Orfe, which is, like the Goldfish and Koi, a member of the Carp family, is a hardy fish, but it jumps a lot. It is not often available.

The price of common Goldfish varieties is usually commensurate with size; individual fish will vary in price from $.15 to $5.00. Goldfish will often exceed 18 inches in length and live more than 25 years.

A Bearded Veiltail Goldfish, an example of the many fancy Goldfish strains being bred today. Photo by Dr. Herbert R. Axelrod.

Beautiful Koi representing a number of color patterns and types mingle in an out-door pool. The white fish at lower right is a female heavily distended with roe. Photo by Dr. Herbert R. Axelrod.

FEEDING: Although it is not necessary to feed Goldfish every day, I feel that feeding with regularity helps to enhance the entertainment value of the fish, since they will learn to take food almost from your hand if they are fed on a regular schedule at the same place every day. But regular feeding does not mean excessive feeding; overfeeding will soon ruin your pond. It is better that the fish always be a little hungry.

One teaspoonful of coarse Goldfish food will satisfy the appetites of six Goldfish averaging four to five inches in length.

Do not feed oatmeal or other cereal, as they tend to foul the water. A good bulk fish food may be purchased inexpensively at your lily supplier or pet shop.

If your pool is over 18 inches deep and is winter-protected you can leave your Goldfish out all winter without worrying about them; they'll be around to greet you next spring. Once ice forms, don't attempt to break it or feed the fish. They will survive the winter with no attention from you.

A Black Moor Goldfish. Photo by Laurence E. Perkins.

Koi, like Goldfish, soon learn to come to the surface to be fed. Photo by Dr. Herbert R. Axelrod.

BREEDING YOUR GOLDFISH: Most Goldfish over 4 inches in length are big enough and old enough to spawn, provided they have gone through one winter. Spawning usually begins in late April, as soon as the weather has had a chance to warm up a little from the winter chill; it continues through June, at which time the water gets too warm to induce further spawning activity. Healthy Goldfish bought and introduced into your pool in early spring will breed readily.

Sexing the fish is not difficult. At spawning time the females become distended with roe and are thus easily distinguished from the males, which remain comparatively slim. Another distinguishing

An informal garden pool set up so that water from the upper level flows into the lower pool in a cascade effect. Photo by Laurence E. Perkins.

mark is the tubercles on the gill covers of the males; these appear at spawning time, but only on the males.

I have found that Goldfish breed best in alkaline water, so concrete pools are ideal, as they usually remain at least slightly alkaline even after the initial curing process gone through when the pool is first set up.

Goldfish lay many eggs. These eggs are not scattered loosely through the water but are laid in plant thickets, preferably near the water's surface; being adhesive, the eggs stick where they are laid. Water Hyacinths have an extensive system of hairy roots which hold

This is an artist's conception of the most popular of the many varieties of Koi.
1. Red and White Calico (Kohaku). 2. White (Shiromuji). 3. Red (Akamuji). 4. Silver-Scale (Ginrin). 5. Tri-Color (Sanshoku). 6. White Tortoise-Shell (Shirobekko). 7. Red Tortoise-Shell (Akabekko). 8. Yellow Mottled (Kiutsushi). 9. Scarlet Mottled (Hiutsushi) 10. White Mottled (Shiroutsushi). 11. Tri-Color Showa (Showa Sanshoku). 12. Light Blue (Asagi). 13. Yellow Carp (Kigoi). 14. Brown Carp (Chagoi). 15. Gold Helmet (Kinkabuto). 16. Silver Helmet (Ginkabuto). 17. Gold (Ogon). 18. Orange-Gold (Orenji-Ogon). 19. Autumn Water (Shusui).

Black is the most extensive color in this Demekin Goldfish.

the eggs well. In addition, the Water Hyacinths may be easily removed, and this is important, because parent Goldfish left alone with their eggs will soon eat them, although some will usually survive.

If you want to raise many fry, remove the egg-holding Water Hyacinths and place both plants and eggs into another pool or a large aquarium containing the same kind of water as is in the pool in which the eggs were laid. At a temperature of 70° the eggs will hatch in 5 to 7 days; generally, the longer the incubation period, the stronger the fry. The newly hatched fry will at first carry their own nourishment in the form of a yolk sac attached to the body, but this will soon be used up. When it is, the fry will need lots of tiny living foods which can be produced by using the commercial "infusoria" tablets available at your dealer's. The fry soon graduate to larger foods and are able to accept finely ground dry food made specifically for feeding infant Goldfish.

Lionhead Goldfish are generally not able to withstand a winter in the pool, but they make wonderful showpieces in the pool during the summer, and may be wintered indoors. Photo by Laurence E. Perkins.

Shubunkins are hardy Goldfish, suitable for pool life, where their multiple colors make them attractive. Photo by Laurence E. Perkins.

The care and breeding of Goldfish is in itself an involved study requiring detailed treatment. I suggest you read the TFH publication *Goldfish*, by Wilfred L. Whitern.

JAPANESE COLORED CARP, "KOI": For centuries Orientals have been famous for their devotion and appreciation of beauty . . . even beauty of small things. Where an American or Englishman would send his sweetheart a dozen roses, an Oriental might send one rose and a few twigs, and the arrangement resulting would be much more beautiful than the dozen roses.

So it was with fishes. First came the Goldfish and its scores of varieties. The earliest Goldfish varieties were mere color varieties. Later, Goldfish with different finnage were developed. Finally, different scale structure and eye development was added to the complex of color and fin variation until hundreds of different Goldfish varieties are available today.

Closeup of water plants adapted to crowded conditions.

Red, gold, white, black . . . many colors are represented in these healthy Koi specimens. Photo by Dr. Herbert R. Axelrod.

This photo was taken through a hole in the ice covering a Goldfish pool in winter. One of these Veiltail Goldfish has developed dropsy. Photo by Laurence E. Perkins.

As the Japanese nation recovered from World War II, more and more gardens appeared, with slowly moving streams, beautiful pools, and artistic landscaping. But the Japanese were tired of the same old Goldfish, and their eyes were turned to the huge Carps that appeared in slightly different color variations from time to time. They called these colorful Carps by the name "Koi," and a tremendous business is currently developing in Japan over the sale and breeding of these beautiful fishes.

Koi are merely fancy varieties of *Carassius carassius*, which the naturalist Linnaeus described about 1758. They have probably been interbred with the Prussian Carp, *Carrassius gibelio*, and with the Common Carp, *Cyprinus carpio*. Some varieties have barbels and some varieties do not. There are scaled Koi and the "German" scaleless Koi. Actually, the so-called scaleless varieties have one or two rows of extremely large scales.

A highly developed Veiltail Goldfish. Photo by Laurence E. Perkins.

The Comet Goldfish is one of the more hardy strains. Photo by Dr. Herbert R. Axelrod.

This water lily is Attraction, a hardy variety. Photo by Paul Stetson.

Castaliflora, a day-blooming tropical variety, moderate in growth. Photo by Paul Stetson.

This is the beautiful Watanai Goldfish.

A magnificent Veiltail Goldfish shown against a background of luxuriant *Vallisneria*.
Photo by Gerhard Budich.

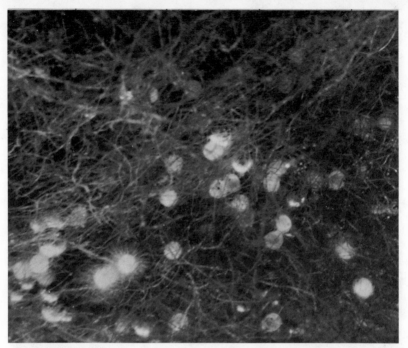

Goldfish eggs laid in a plant thicket. At least two of the eggs have been attacked by fungus. Photo by Laurence E. Perkins.

So many color varieties have already been developed that the Japanese have run out of names for them. No English names have yet been assigned, and the names used here are used only for convenience. Where known, the Japanese name has been given under the photos. Though the names of the various color varieties are obscure at this time, the methods of care and breeding are well known.

Adult Koi are definitely outdoor fish. They do best in temperate climates where the water in a pool three feet deep won't freeze solid in the winter. Because they are bottom-feeding fish, they are dirty, and they do best in running water. Over-feeding is the greatest cause of their problems, and they should be fed once every two days after they are six months old. Younger fish should be fed daily.

Needless to say, Koi do best on pelletized Goldfish food, frozen brine shrimp, and *Tubifex* worms, but the economics of feeding fish that grow to two feet long and eat two pounds a week demands that the fish's diet suffer a bit to make Koi economical pets.

H. C. Haarstick, the most popular night blooming tropical. Photo by Paul Stetson.

The flower of the Water Hyacinth, *Eichhornia crassipes*. Photo by Paul Stetson.

The Wakin is an example of a Goldfish in which body and color conformation is more important than the development of extensive finnage.

Pond fish food suits them ideally if you throw them some frozen brine shrimp one or twice a month. They are ideal pool pets and soon learn to accept food from your fingers. The warmer the water the more active and colorful the Koi is, but the most beautiful require a "freeze" for a few months.

The care and breeding of Koi is exactly the same as that of Goldfish. The males develop nuptial tubercles on their gill covers and the females become plump with eggs. This all happens in the springtime, around March or April in the Northern Hemisphere. The breeders lay their eggs in the roots of floating Water Hyacinth; unless they have been properly fed, they will start eating them almost as soon as they have laid them.

The Japanese use purely aesthetic standards for their Koi. The most colorful fish with the brightest colors and the greatest number of colors (a four-colored fish is a rare one), is the best. Purity of color is also prized. A white Koi is valuable only if it is pure white. One black scale ruins it. Yet a white Koi with some red, black, and brown, regardless of how much of each color, is very highly prized. Koi with very contrasting colors are extremely valuable, most especially the metallic gold Koi. Yes, as unbelievable as it sounds, they have Koi with a solid gold coloration that actually glitters like gold! Koi are highly recommended for the garden pool . . . and small varieties do well in the home aquarium.

These are young Bubble-eye Goldfish at four weeks of age. Photo by Laurance E. Perkins.

Pistia stratiotes, Water Lettuce, has an extensive root network, but this plant is not as good a receiver of Goldfish and Koi spawn as the Water Hyancinth. Photo by Duncan Sculthorpe.

This *Nymphaea* species was photographed in its home waters in South America; it is not a pool-raised plant. Photo by Harald Schultz.

These are just two of the many styles of concrete pools available. Photo by Paul Stetson.

August Koch, one of the day-blooming tropical varieties, has large flowers. Photo by Paul Stetson.

The Kinranshi Goldfish, like the Lionhead, completely lacks a dorsal fin.

Nymphaea species, showing floating and emergent foliage and open flowers. Photo by Duncan Sculthorpe.

The Pearlscale Goldfish is one of the rarer and more costly Goldfish. Photo by Laurence E. Perkins.

This is *Carassius carassius*, one of the plain fishes from which today's beautiful Koi specimens have been developed. Photo by G. J. M. Timmerman.

The flower of this *Nelumbium* species rises above the plant on a seemingly fragile bloomstalk. Photo by Paul Stetson.

Afterglow, a tropical day blooming pink lily. Photo by Paul Stetson.

SUMMER CARE AND MAINTENANCE OF THE POOL

The sun is friend to beautiful lilies and unsightly algae alike, and since algae reproduce more quickly than the flowering plants which you are cultivating, your pool might become overrun until the flowering plants get a good start and eliminate the algae by drawing the algae's nutriment from the water and cutting off the amount of light available.

Don't empty your pool to get rid of algae; this does no good, because the algae will thrive in new water, and you will only start the

Water Hyacinths are useful as receivers of fish spawn and for their help in cutting down the amount of algae in the pool. Photo by Duncan Sculthorpe.

cycle again. Rapid growers, such as Water Hyacinth, will help kill off the algae, and once your pool clears it will remain clear all summer long. Of the chemical preparations formulated to kill algae, potassium permanganate is best. Some very effective chemical preparations are marketed in ready-to-use form, so you don't have to mix the chemicals yourself.

Since very few insects attack water lilies, insect control is not much of a problem. Aphids, one of the few bugs likely to give trouble, are softbodied and can usually be destroyed by playing a strong stream of water on them. Nicotine sulphate may also be used, but only if there are no fishes or other animals in the pool. The non-vegetative pool life must also be protected from sprays used in other parts of the garden. Cover your pool if it becomes necessary to spray around it, and cover it especially well when your neighbourhood is to be sprayed for mosquitoes.

In the process of growth, plants shed their old leaves. These can be a source of trouble in the pool, besides looking bad, so get rid of them. A periodic cleanup is a good idea.

Gonnere, a double water lily suitable for use in small pools, where space is at a premium. Photo by Paul Stetson.

Comanche Hara, a large lily suited to fairly large pools, changes color as it ages.
Photo by Paul Stetson.

This is a Comet Goldfish, one of the hardiest Goldfish varieties for a garden pool.

ORDERING FISHES AND PLANTS

Until only a few years ago it was usual to ship Goldfish in metal cans containing up to 15 gallons of water; even in this amount of water, only a few fish could be shipped, and the chances of fatalities were great. With the advent of the use of polyethylene bags, however, both Goldfish and tropical fishes can be shipped long distances with little risk, especially when pure oxygen and fish tranquilizers are added to the shipping bag. Using these refinements, I have shipped as many as 500 small Goldfish in 3 gallons of water, with good results.

Goldfish may now be shipped in the mails, or by rail and air express services. Large shipments may even be sent by air freight. However your shipment is sent, you can be reasonably sure that it will arrive in good shape. It is best to order your Goldfish in the early part of spring, although insulated shipping boxes make shipping possible throughout the year. Of course, you can always go and pick up your fish yourself if you are within driving distance of your supplier.

Male (left) and female Celestial Goldfish in typical pose during "chasing" phase of mating act, just prior to spawning. Photo by Laurence E. Perkins.

When your Goldfish arrive they should be floated in your pool or aquarium for about half an hour, with the shipping bag left fully inflated. If there are dead fish in the bag, however, open the bag at once and release the fish into the new water.

Plants are shipped by the same media as Goldfish, but they are usually packed in sphagnum and wrapped in wet paper. It is always best to send extra postage to your supplier so that your plants will be sent air express. The plants are best left in their original packings until you are ready to plant them. Most plants need a little time to get used to their new surroundings and will not do well at first, but they recover quickly, more quickly than terrestrial plants. Remove all dead and withered leaves, but don't be too hasty to discard a plant which seems to be in poor condition.

Hardy plants shipped in spring will generally still be in a dormant state and will not look as impressive as those shipped later in the season. Also, many tall plants have to have their tops cut off to accommodate them to the shipping cartons, so don't be in a hurry to blame your shipper for sending you inferior plants. Reliable suppliers allow reasonable claims for unsatisfactory plants, and no shipper who intends to stay in business will knowingly send you bad plants. Leave it up to your supplier to get the plants to you in time to give you a full summer's enjoyment of them. Hardy varieties are usually shipped after April 15 and tropical varieties after May 30, except in southern areas, where planting may be done up to a month earlier in either case.

During the shipping season your supplier is a very busy man and cannot always answer correspondence as thoroughly or as promptly as he would like, so co-operate with him. You'll soon find that his knowledge and experience can be counted on to be put to your use in arranging your water garden in a way that will maximize your pleasure from it at the lowest cost to you. Enjoy your acquaintance with your supplier; most of all, enjoy your new hobby. It's yours for a long time to come.

Isabelle Pring, the purest white tropical day blooming water lily. Photo by Paul Stetson.